THE GOFF

THE GOFF

Facsimiles of Three Editions
of the Heroi-Comical
Poem by

THOMAS MATHISON

Introductory Essays by

Joseph S. F. Murdoch

&

Stephen Ferguson

UNITED STATES GOLF ASSOCIATION

1981

PREFACE

WHEN first published in 1743, *The Goff* was the first separately printed book devoted entirely to golf. This premier volume of the literature of the game was published twice again before the end of the eighteenth century, in 1763 and 1793. Since that time this rarity has reappeared only in three golf anthologies of a century ago. Today the United States Golf Association presents this first modern edition of the poem in facsimiles of all three of the eighteenth-century editions.

The Library of the Association at Golf House is the only collection known to contain all three editions of *The Goff*, thanks to the generosity of the late O. M. Leland, who gave his entire golf library to the Association in 1957. It is from these copies that the facsimiles have been made.

The Association plans these facsimiles to be the first publication in a series of reprintings of major books in the literature of golf. It is hoped that by republishing these important but difficult-to-find texts, the Association will not only maintain the fine traditions of golf but will promote greater knowledge of the history of the game.

By republishing a series of great golf books, the Association also hopes to promote awareness of the Library at Golf House as well as other great collections of golf books in this country.

Perhaps surprising to some, the earliest printed reference to golf dates from 1566. Since that time an extensive literature of golf has developed. A bibliography of the game, *The Library of Golf 1743–1966* by Joseph S. F. Murdoch, has nearly 900 entries. Many of the rare and early books listed in that bibliography are to be found at Golf House and will be the source of future books in this series.

Several people are to be acknowledged for bringing about this book. All are grateful to the book collectors—in particular, O. M. Leland and

Max H. Behr—who collected and preserved these rare editions prior to their coming to the Library at Golf House. To Joseph S. F. Murdoch and to Stephen Ferguson, who first suggested the idea, we extend deep appreciation for their introductions. Also to be thanked is Robert M. Lunny, a member of the Association Museum Committee and Director Emeritus of The New Jersey Historical Society, for his editorial assistance. Two staff members also deserve the thanks of the Association: Janet Seagle, Librarian and Museum Curator, and John M. Morris, Director, Communications, for developing this entire project.

HARRY W. EASTERLY, JR.
Senior Executive Director
United States Golf Association
Far Hills, New Jersey
November 1981

THE PLACE OF *THE GOFF*
IN THE LITERATURE OF GOLF

IN the introduction to *Golfiana Miscellanea*, published in 1887, the editor, James Lindsay Stewart, suggested:

Along with the more widely extended attachment to the game, there has been also a largely-increasing interest in its literature and historical associations. The literary productions on the subject are not very numerous, and such as they are, whether historical, poetical, or descriptive, all, except such as may have been published within a few years, are scarce and difficult to get.

Stewart explained that his reason for bringing out his anthology was this scarcity alluded to and the desirability to produce a reprint of these scarcities "at a low price, and so within the reach of any one." Unfortunately for today's collector of golfiana, his book, too, has become "scarce and difficult to get." Even more difficult to get is the first book Stewart selected to reprint, a mock epic poem by Thomas Mathison, *The Goff*.

The United States Golf Association, in making available this very old and historic poem, offers a great service to golf historians and golf collectors around the world.

The reference to golf collectors is deliberate for it is because of such enthusiasts, relatively few in number down through the many years golf has been played, that such treasures as *The Goff* are still with us. Viewed as somewhat eccentric citizens of the world of golf, perhaps somewhat like the very few golfers who still play with a red ball over snow-covered courses, the collector finds a certain fascination in searching out and accumulating golfing books and memorabilia. It is a game he plays which brings him as much satisfaction as sinking a long putt or hitting a towering drive. And when aging muscles and perhaps increasing girth no longer allow outstanding play, the pleasure derived from his collection eases the frustration.

There are very few references to the game of golf before 1743. The earliest references are the well-known Acts of Scottish Parliament, which banned the playing of "golfe." These various Acts were issued in 1457, 1471, and again in 1491. They became the first *printed* references when published in one volume in Edinburgh in 1566.

Because the above references are legal in nature, it is commonly agreed that *The Muses Threnodie*, a book written by Henry Adamson and published in Edinburgh in 1638, includes the first published mention of the game addressed to the general public. This book contained a "variety of pleasant Poetical Descriptions, Moral Instructions, Historical Narrations, and Divine Observations." The lines on golf were not, sadly, under "Divine Observations" but rather among the "pleasant Poetical Descriptions." There are only two lines:

> And yee, my clubs, you must no more prepare
> To make your bals flee whistling in the aire.

These references, one observes, are of Scottish origin.

The first English reference is contained in a book published in 1661 in London. This book, *Instructions to a Son*, was written by the Marquess of Argyle and the lines referring to golf are in prose:

Tennis is not in use amongst us, but only in our Capital City [Edinburgh] but in lieu of that, you have the excellent recreation of Goff-ball than which truly I do not know a better.

Another of the very early references was a diary written in 1687 and 1688. It contains numerous references to golf, which O. M. Leland explains:

In the Edinburgh newspaper, *The Scotsman*, for August 2, 1938, there appeared an article by Dr. Henry W. Meikle, Librarian of the National Library of Scotland, announcing the discovery among the manuscripts in the library of an item of special significance to the history and literature of golf. It consisted of a diary. . . .

Meikle pursued his research and subsequently identified the diarist as Thomas Kincaid, a young medical student at the University of Edinburgh. The diary was published in *The Book of the Old Edinburgh Club*, Volume 17, 1949.

8

To the golf reporter of today, it may be of some interest that the first mention of the game in the daily press appeared in 1724 when an account of a match played on Leith Links was reported in an Edinburgh newspaper.

Aside from these few and other fragmentary references, *The Goff* stands unique as a substantial publication because it would be another eighty years before another book, exclusively devoted to the subject, would be published: *Rules of the Thistle Club*, in 1824. Standing alone in a century of silence, it is little wonder that we, today, would like to know more about this very first golf book.

Two golf collectors especially are important to the history of *The Goff*. The first is C. B. Clapcott, an English collector who before his death in 1956 amassed a wonderful golf library that included most, if not all, the rarities in the game's literature. The second is the late O. M. Leland, an enthusiastic collector from St. Paul, Minnesota. He, too, owned an impressive library, which was the first major acquisition of the United States Golf Association Library when Leland donated his collection to the Association in 1957. Both of these gentlemen were great scholars of golf literature and each did some writing on the subject.

Clapcott's writing was more extensive than was Leland's. A number of copies of the former's papers have found their way into some collections. It is probable that Clapcott wrote them for his own enlightenment and gave away copies to his close friends. All of them are interesting for their meticulous research and for the conclusions he reached on golf subjects which until then had not been investigated.

Among the most fascinating of these papers is *The Goff: An Heroi-Comical Poem in Three Cantos; A Commentary by C. B. C.*, which Clapcott wrote in 1946. The original typescript of this work is in the Department of Manuscripts of the National Library of Scotland, where it hides under its assigned number, MS 3999. Mathison's poem is typed on the right-hand pages and Clapcott's commentary to relevant points in the poem is typed on the facing left-hand pages.

This commentary was first brought to my attention by my son, who was doing research for his doctorate at the National Library in 1975, and some months later I read it with fascination and greatest pleasure. I was elated with his "discovery." I use that word only because I had never heard of the commentary before and to my knowledge no golf publication had ever mentioned it. I can only assume that it lay in the files of the Library

9

unnoticed and unread for many years. My immediate thought was to obtain a copy of it and to bring it to the attention of other collectors around the world but this idea was abandoned because of Library policy.

Enter O. M. Leland and yet another discovery. In recent years the library collection of the United States Golf Association has been recatalogued. In doing so, parts of the Leland collection that had not been catalogued before turned up and there was a photostatic copy of the commentary.

Leland was always meticulous in making notations of his acquisitions, and from such a note we learn that he acquired his copy in 1952, some six years after it had been written. We know also that Leland had met with Clapcott in Great Britain on the occasion of Leland's one trip there in 1947, so we must presume that the two scholars corresponded in the ensuing years, resulting finally in the American's acquisition of the commentary. Also noted on the cover of the photostat in Leland's distinctive hand is the note "From the Nat'l Library of Scotland." Now, with the great advantage of having a copy in hand, we can offer Clapcott's elucidation of *The Goff* to the modern reader.

The 1793 edition as described in Part II of this introduction enabled Clapcott to proceed with his minute examination of the various identity clues that are offered in the poem and Peter Hill's "Notes and Illustrations" were of great help to the Englishman.

It would be difficult to prove or disprove Clapcott's statement in his foreword that "hitherto, it has been thought that the poem was an account in verse of an imaginary contest between two imaginary players." The notes of the third edition of 1793 certainly indicate that the poem did, indeed, report an actual match but there is little question that Clapcott contributed greatly to painting a fuller picture of what actually happened as it was described in the poem.

As to the match itself, it is played on Leith Links . . .

> Who from Edina's towers, his peaceful home,
> In quest of fame o'er Letha's plains did roam.
> CANTO I, LINES 3–4

and starting about 12 noon . . .

> And warm'd the earth with genial noontide ray.
> CANTO I, LINE 36

10

lasted until the late afternoon . . .

> The Scotian fields, and lengthens out the shades;
> CANTO III, LINE 8

in the late spring of the year . . .

> And frisking lambkins dance around the God,
> CANTO III, LINE 84.

The stake, or bet, is nearly a quart of punch . . .

> The Vanquish'd hero for the victor fills
> A mighty bowl containing thirty gills;
> With noblest liquor is the bowl replete,
> CANTO I, LINES 85–87

and to give the story away, the author of the poem lost . . .

> For him Pygmalion must the bowl prepare,
> CANTO III, LINE 141

One player is "Castalio" and Clapcott explains that he is Alexander Dunning, a bookseller from Edinburgh and apparently ranked among the better golfers of his time. His opponent, the author, is "Pygmalion," ("Small is his size, but dauntless is his heart") and Clapcott, at some labor, eventually points out that the two were brothers-in-law. What better reason than that to have a match?

The match, itself, is not described in any great detail. We know that Castalio won the honor . . .

> Then great Castalio his whole force collects,
> and on the orb a noble blow directs.

to be followed by . . .

> Next in his turn Pygmalion strikes the globe:
> On the upper half descends the erring club;

Or, as we would say today, he topped it!

But golf, as we all know, is a funny game even though, as an ancient once said, "twas not meant to be!" After three (of the four) rounds, or 15 holes (Leith in 1743 was a five-hole course!), Pygmalion is three down and we all know that the opponent down three with five to play is a dangerous opponent indeed. Sure enough, the two players come to "the last great hole" all even and Pygmalion has the honor.

The play at the last hole is described at some length but in the end, Castalio holes his approach and Pygmalion ("from the hole scarce twice two clubs' lengths . . . feebly tips the ball with trembling hands") missed the even and lost the match.

It is of interest to note that many years later, in 1890, Andrew Lang, another of the great Scottish classical scholars, was to refer to the poem in the chapter Lang contributed to the volume in the Badminton Library on golf. Lang's conclusion as to the outcome of the match, however, is not the same as Clapcott's. He deemed it halved.

Here, then, is *The Goff*, the first of a long and sometimes noble shelf of books written about a rather simple game which began in a tiny corner of a rather small country and now attracts millions of enthusiasts around the world. *The Goff* has been described as "spirited," "of the greatest importance," "the real classic" (of golf literature), "a highly desirable item" and "the hall-mark of a fine golfing library."

The huge library that followed this brave, thin volume includes many treasures and promises great delight for anyone who will devote a bit of time to the reading of them.

At one other time, I quoted one of the finest of today's many fine golf writers, Herbert Warren Wind, and because it is applicable here, I have no hesitancy in using it again.

Over the years a vast body of writing has accumulated which far surpasses any other game's for sheer quantity. While a large part of this outpouring falls a good distance short of that standard of writing we call literature, no other game has acquired a literature that compares with golf's. Men write extremely well about it and sometimes wonderfully.

JOSEPH S. F. MURDOCH, *Co-Founder*
The Golf Collectors Society

PRINTING AND LITERARY HISTORY OF *THE GOFF*

ALTHOUGH the poem was published anonymously, it is generally accepted that the author of *The Goff* was Thomas Mathison, born on August 13, 1721, the last of eight children born to William Mathison, merchant, and Elizabeth Mark, his spouse. Early in life he was a lawyer's clerk and also attempted a career as a writer. "He was licensed by the Presbytery of Dalkeith, November 1st, 1748, and for a time officiated in a Presbyterian congregation in the North of England. In September, 1750, he was ordained assistant and successor to William Hepburn, minister of Inverkeilor; and was translated to the second charge of the parish of Brechin in July, 1754. He died June 19, 1760."[1] In the year of his death he published his *Sacred Ode . . . Occasioned by the Late Successes Attending the British Arms*, a poem referring to the French and Indian War in America, during which Quebec was captured by the English on September 18, 1759.

At the time he wrote the poem, Mathison was a young man, about the age of twenty-two. He calls *The Goff* a "heroi-comical poem" and it is indeed what we today call a mock epic. As the reader of these facsimiles will learn, the poem depicts a golf match with all the grandeur of a battle between mythical heroes of ancient Greece and Rome.

The intent of the poem is satiric and ironic; there are always two levels of meaning on which the poem operates. On the one hand, there is the literal action of the match between the mythic heroes; on the other, veiled behind the names are real people and events. In the mock epic traditions of the English speaking writers of the eighteenth century, the poem follows closely the conventions of the day. The opening line, "Goff, and the *Man*, I sing. . . ," echoes the opening of the Iliad and the Aeneid. The muse, in

1. J. L. Stewart (ed.), *Golfiana Miscellanea* (Glasgow, 1887).

this case Golfinia, is invoked to inspire the poet; the players are given classical names "Pygmalion" and "Castalio" although they are ordinary Scots; the match builds to a final battle at the last hole.

In *The Goff*, Mathison is Pygmalion, who in classical literature was the legendary King of Cyprus who fell in love with a beautiful statue which he had carved in ivory. Pygmalion prayed to Aphrodite that she give him a wife resembling the statue. In turn, Aphrodite gave life to the statue and Pygmalion married her. In the eighteenth century the story of Pygmalion was well known, and one can assume from Mathison's use of the name for himself that he also wanted the entire story to apply to him. As an aspiring writer, he wanted his poetry to come to life.

Pygmalion's opponent in *The Goff* is Castalio. Castalio has been identified as Alexander Dunning, an Edinburgh bookseller who first entered the trade in 1726. Although it is impossible to find an indubitable correspondent for this name in classical literature, it is evident that Mathison adopted the name from the adjectival form *castalius*—meaning of or relating to *Castalia*, which was the fountain on Parnassus sacred to the Muses and Apollo. In the English of Mathison's day, *castalian* meant poetic and a *castalianist* was a poet. Hence, by calling the bookseller Dunning "Castalio" Mathison is glorifying him as the inspiration of poets. And with such a name Mathison is using a double entendre. Dunning was not only the inspiration of this particular poem but as a publisher was the supporter of his writers. It was the function of booksellers to pay authors for their works; there were no publishers in the eighteenth century as we know them today.

One cannot help but sense the good humor of the poem and assume that Dunning and Mathison were on friendly terms. And, indeed, available evidence shows that, in general, writers and booksellers (their employers or potential employers) had a cordial relationship during the eighteenth century.[2]

Other characters in the poem have been identified as members of the Honourable Company of Golfers.

As mentioned, *The Goff* was first published at Edinburgh in 1743. It was

2. For commentary on the poem and a study of its place in the comic poetry of its day see Richmond P. Bond, *English Burlesque Poetry 1700–1750* (Cambridge: Harvard University Press, 1932), pp. 414–417. On the relationship between writer and bookseller, see A. S. Collins, *Authorship in the Days of Johnson: Being a Study of the Relation between Author, Patron, Publisher and Public, 1726–1780* (London: George Routledge & Sons, 1928).

advertised for sale in the May, 1743, issue of *The Scots Magazine*, a journal published by James Cochran, who, as seen in the facsimiles, printed the poem and according to the advertisement, had copies for sale at four pence each.

The second edition of *The Goff* was published in Leith, where the match was played, in 1763 by James Reid, bookseller. Its price was also four pence. The third edition was published at Edinburgh in 1793 by Peter Hill and contained "A Few Notes and Illustrations." It was dedicated to "All Lovers of Goff in Europe, Asia, Africa, and America" and, among other things, it lists the names of the "Caledonian Chiefs" alluded to in the poem. In the appendix to the third edition also are two poems added by the publisher. They are "Song in Praise of Goff" and "The Goffers." The former was later to be known as "The Golfer's Garland." Following each title is the name of a tune, leading one to think it was meant to be sung. In the nineteenth century, the poem was reprinted in *Poems on Golf*, Edinburgh, 1867, in *Golf a Royal and Ancient Game*, Edinburgh, 1875, and in *Golfiana Miscellanea*, edited by J. L. Stewart, Glasgow, 1887.

All three editions of the eighteenth century are very rare. For the first edition, the following copies are known: British Library, London; Bodleian Library, Oxford; National Library of Scotland, Edinburgh; Mitchell Library, Glasgow; Yale University Library, New Haven; University of North Carolina, Chapel Hill; Henry E. Huntington Library, San Marino, California; United States Golf Association Library, Far Hills, New Jersey; and Ralph W. Miller Library, Industry Hills, California. The second edition is found in the British Library, the Library of the United States Golf Association and the Professional Golfers Association of America Library in Palm Beach Gardens, Florida. The third edition is found in the National Library of Scotland and the library of the Association, the only institution known to possess all three editions.

The facsimiles of the first two editions are reproduced in full size. For reasons of space, the third edition is reproduced eighty per cent of full size.

STEPHEN FERGUSON
Curator of Rare Books
Princeton University Library

1743

THE
GOFF.

AN

Heroi-Comical Poem.

IN

Three CANTOS.

THE
GOUT.

AN

Heroi-Comical Poem.

IN

Three CANTOS.

T H E

G O F F.

A N

Heroi - Comical Poem.

I N

Three C A N T O S.

Cætera, quæ vacuas tenuiſſent carmina mentes,
Omnia jam volgata.   VIRG.

E D I N B U R G H:

Printed by J. C O C H R A N and C O M P A N Y.
M D C C X L I I I.

[*Price Four Pence.*]

THE
G O F F.
CANTO I.

GOFF, and the *Man*, I sing, who, em'lous,
          plies
      The jointed club; whose balls invade the
          skies;
Who from *Edina*'s tow'rs, his peaceful home,
In quest of fame o'er *Letha*'s plains did roam.
Long toil'd the hero, on the verdant field,   5
Strain'd his stout arm the weighty club to wield;
Such toils it cost, such labours to obtain
The bays of conquest, and the bowl to gain.

(4)

O thou GOLFINIA, Goddeſs of theſe plains,
Great patroneſs of GOFF, indulge my ſtrains; 10
Whether beneath the *thorn-tree* ſhade you lie,
Or from *Mercerian* tow'rs the game ſurvey,
Or 'round the green the flying ball you chaſe,
Or make your bed in ſome hot ſandy *face*:
Leave your much lov'd abode, inſpire his lays 15
Who ſings of GOFF, and ſings thy fav'rite's praiſe.

North from *Edina* eight furlongs and more
Lies that fam'd field, on *Fortha*'s ſounding ſhore.
Here, *Caledonian* Chiefs for health reſort,
Confirm their ſinews by the manly ſport. 20
Macd——d and unmatch'd *D——ple* ply
Their pond'rous weapons, and the green defy;
R—tt—y for ſkill, and *C—ſe* for ſtrength renown'd,
St—rt and *L—ſly* beat the ſandy ground,
And *Br—n* and *Alſt—n*, Chiefs well known to fame,
And numbers more the Muſe forbears to name. 26
Gigantic *B—gg—r* here full oft is ſeen,
Like huge Behemoth on an *Indian* green;

His

His bulk enormous scarce can 'scape the eyes,

Amaz'd spectators wonder how he plies.   30

Yea here great F——s, patron of the just,

The dread of villains, and the good man's trust,

When spent with toils in serving human kind,

His body recreates, and unbends his mind.

    Bright *Phœbus* now, had measur'd half the day   35

And warm'd the earth with genial noontide ray :

Forth rush'd *Castalio* and his daring foe,

Both arm'd with clubs, and eager for the blow.

Of finest ash *Castalio*'s shaft was made,

Pond'rous with lead, and fenc'd with horn the head,

(The work of *Dickson*, who in *Letha* dwells,   41

And in the art of making clubs excels),

Which late beneath great *Claro*'s arm did bend,

But now is wielded by his greater friend.

    Not with more fury *Norris* cleav'd the main,   45

To pour his thund'ring arms on guilty *Spain* ;

Nor with more haste brave *Haddock* bent his course,

To guard *Minorca* from *Iberian* force :

                               Than

Than thou, intrepid hero, urg'd thy way,
O'er roads and fands, impatient for the fray.　50

 With equal warmth *Pygmalion* faft purfu'd,
(With courage oft are little wights endow'd),
'Till to GOLFINIA's downs the heroes came,
The fcene of combat, and the field of fame.

 Upon a verdant bank, by FLORA grac'd,　55
Two fifter Fairies found the Goddefs plac'd;
Propp'd by her fnowy hand her head reclin'd,
Her curling locks hung waving in the wind.
She eyes intent the confecrated green,
Crowded with waving clubs, and vot'ries keen,　60
And hears the prayers of youths to her addrefs'd
And from the hollow face relieves the ball diftrefs'd.
On either fide the fprightly Dryads fat,
And entertain'd the Goddefs with their chat.

 Firft VERDURILLA, thus: O rural Queen!　65
What Chiefs are thofe that drive along the green?
With brandifh'd clubs the mighty heroes threat,
Their eager looks fortell a keen debate.

To

To whom GOLFINIA: Nymph, your eyes behold
Pygmalion stout, *Castalio* brave and bold.   70
From silver *Ierna's* banks *Castalio* came,
But first on *Andrean* plains he courted fame.
His fire, a Druid, taught (one day of seven)
The paths of virtue, the sure road to heaven.
In *Pictish* capital the good man past   75
His virtuous life, and there he breath'd his last.
The son now dwells in fair *Edina's* town,
And on our sandy plains pursues renown.
See low *Pygmalion*, skill'd in GOFFING art,
Small is his size, but dauntless is his heart: 80
Fast by a desk in *Edin's* domes he sits,
With *saids* and *sicklikes* length'ning out the writs.
For no mean prize the rival Chiefs contend,
But full rewards the victor's toils attend.
The vanquish'd hero for the victor fills   85
A mighty bowl containing thirty gills;
With noblest liquor is the bowl replete;
Here sweets and acids, strength and weakness meet.

From

From *Indian* isles the strength and sweetness flow,

And *Tagus'* banks their golden fruits bestow, 90

Cold *Caledonia's* lucid streams controul

The fiery spirits, and fulfil the bowl.

For *Albion's* peace and *Albion's* friends they pray,

And drown in *punch* the labours of the day.

The Goddess spoke, and thus GAMBOLIA pray'd:

Permit to join in brave *Pygmalion's* aid, 96

O'er each deep road the hero to sustain,

And guide his ball to the desired plain.

To this the Goddess of the manly sport:

Go, and be thou that daring Chief's support: 100

Let VERDURILLA be *Castalio's* stay:

I from this flow'ry seat will view the fray.

She said: the nymphs trip nimbly o'er the green,

And to the combatants approach unseen.

The End of the first Canto.

CAN-

CANTO II.

YE rural powers that on these plains preside,
  Ye nymphs that dance on *Fortha's* flow'ry side,
Assist the Muse that in your fields delights,
And guide her course in these uncommon flights.
But chief, thee, O GOLFINIA! I implore;   5
High as thy balls instruct my Muse to soar:
So may thy green forever crowded be,
And balls on balls invade the azure sky.

Now at that hole the Chiefs begin the game,
Which from the neighb'ring *thorn-tree* takes its name;
Ardent they grasp the ball-compelling clubs,   11
And stretch their arms t'attack the little globes.
Not as our warriors brandish'd dreadful arms,
When fierce *Bellona* sounded war's alarms,
When conqu'ring *Cromwel* stain'd fair *Eska's* flood
And soak'd her banks with *Caledonian* blood;   16
Or when our bold ancestors madly fought,
And Clans engag'd for trifles or for nought.

B   That

That *Fury* now from our bless'd fields is driv'n,
To scourge unhappy nations doom'd by heav'n. 20
Let *Kouli Kan* destroy the fertile East,
Victorious *Vernon* thunder in the West;
Let horrid war involve perfidious *Spain*,
And GEORGE assert his empire o'er the Main:
But on our plains *Britannia*'s sons engage, 25
And void of ire the sportive war they wage.

Lo, tatter'd *Irus*, who their armour bears,
Upon the green two little pyr'mids rears;
On these they place two balls with careful eye,
That with *Clarinda*'s breasts for colour vye, 30
The work of *Bobson*; who with matchless art
Shapes the firm hide, connecting ev'ry part,
Then in a socket sets the well-stitch'd void,
And thro' the eylet drives the downy tide;
Crowds urging Crowds the forceful brogue impels, 35
The feathers harden and the Leather swells;
He crams and sweats, yet crams and urges more,
Till scarce the turgid globe contains its store:

The

The dreaded falcon's pride here blended lies
With pigeons glossy down of various dyes;   40
The lark's small pinions join the common stock,
And yellow glory of the martial cock.

    Soon as *Hyperion* gilds old *Andrea*'s spires,
From bed the artist to his cell retires;
With bended back, there plies his steely awls,   45
And shapes, and stuffs, and finishes the balls.
But when the glorious God of day has driv'n
His flaming chariot down the steep of heav'n,
He ends his labour, and with rural strains
Enchants the lovely maids and weary swains: 50
As thro' the streets the blythsome piper plays,
In antick dance they answer to his lays;
At ev'ry pause the ravish'd crowd acclaim,
And rend the skies with tuneful *Bobson*'s name.
Not more rewarded was old *Amphion*'s song;   55
That rear'd a town, and this drags one along.
Such is fam'd *Bobson*, who in *Andrea* thrives,
And such the balls each vig'rous hero drives.

First, bold *Castalio*, ere he struck the blow,
Lean'd on his club, and thus address'd his foe : 60
Dares weak *Pygmalion* this stout arm defy,
Which brave *Matthias* doth with terror try?
Strong as he is, *Moravio* owns my might,
Distrusts his vigour, and declines the fight.
Renown'd *Clephanio* I constrain'd to yield, 65
And drove the haughty vet'ran from the field.
Weak is thine arm, rash youth, thy courage vain ;
Vanquish'd, with shame you'll curse the fatal plain.
The half-struck balls your weak endeavours mock,
Slowly proceed, and soon forget the stroke. 70
Not so the orb eludes my thund'ring force :
Thro' fields of air it holds its rapid course,
Swift as the balls from martial engines driv'n,
Streams like a comet thro' the arch of heav'n.

Vaunter, go on, (*Pygmalion* thus replies) ; 75
Thine empty boasts with justice I despise.
Hadst thou the strength *Goliah*'s spear to wield,
Like its great master thunder on the field,

And

And with that ftrength *C—ll—d—n*'s matchlefs art,
Not one unmanly thought fhould daunt my heart.
He faid, and fign'd to *Irus*; who, before, 81
With frequent warnings fill'd the founding fhore.

Then great *Caftalio* his whole force collects,
And on the orb a noble blow directs.
Swift as a thought the ball obedient flies, 85
Sings high in air, and feems to cleave the fkies;
Then on the level plain its fury fpends;
And *Irus* to the Chief the welcome tidings fends.
Next in his turn *Pygmalion* ftrikes the globe:
On th' upper half defcends the erring club; 90
Along the green the ball confounded fcours;
No lofty flight the ill-fped ftroke impow'rs.

Thus, when the trembling hare defcries the hounds,
She from her whinny manfion fwiftly bounds;
O'er hills and fields fhe fcours, outftrips the wind;
The hounds and huntfmen follow far behind. 96

GAMBOLIA now afforded timely aid;
She o'er the fand the fainting ball convey'd,

Re-

Renew'd its force, and urg'd it on its way,

Till on the fummit of the hill it lay.   100

Now all on fire the Chiefs their orbs purfue,

With the next ftroke the orbs their flight renew :

Thrice round the green they urge the whizzing ball,

And thrice three holes to great *Caftalio* fall;

The other fix *Pygmalion* bore away,   105

And fav'd a while the honours of the day.

Had fome brave champion of the fandy field

The Chiefs attended, and the game beheld;

With ev'ry ftroke his wonder had increaft,

And em'lous fires had kindled in his breaft.   110

The End of the fecond Canto.

CAN-

CANTO III.

HArmonious Nine, that from *Parnaſſus* view
  The ſubject world, and all that's done below;
Who from oblivion ſnatch the patriot's name,
And to the ſtars extol the hero's fame,
Bring each your lyre, and to my ſong repair,   5
Nor think GOLFINIA's train below the Muſes care.

  Declining *Sol* with milder beams invades
The *Scotian* fields, and lengthens out the ſhades;
Haſtes to ſurvey the conquer'd golden plains,
Where captive *Indians* mourn in *Spaniſh* chains;   10
To gild the waves where hapleſs *Hoſier* dy'd,
Where *Vernon* late proud *Bourbon*'s force defy'd,
Triumphant rode along the wat'ry plain,
Britannia's glory and the ſcourge of *Spain*.

  Still from her ſeat the *Power* of *GOFF* beheld
Th' unweary'd heroes toiling on the field: 16
The light-foot Fairies in their labours ſhare,
Each nymph her hero ſeconds in the war;

Pyg-

Pygmalion and GAMBOLIA there appear,

And VERDURILLA with *Caſtalio* here. 20

The Goddeſs ſaw, and op'd the book of Fate,

To ſearch the iſſue of the grand debate.

Bright ſilver plates the ſacred leaves infold,

Bound with twelve ſhining claſps of ſolid gold.

The wond'rous book contains the fate of all 25

That lift the club, and ſtrike the miſſive ball;

Myſterious rhymes that thro' the pages flow,

The paſt, the preſent, and the future ſhow.

GOLFINIA reads the Fate-foretelling lines,

And ſoon the ſequel of the war divines; 30

Sees conqueſt doom'd *Caſtalio*'s toils to crown,

Pygmalion doom'd ſuperior might to own.

Then at her ſide VICTORIA ſtraight appears,

Her ſiſter Goddeſs, arbitreſs of wars.

Upon her head a wreath of bays ſhe wore, 35

And in her hand a laurel ſceptre bore;

Anxious to know the will of Fate ſhe ſtands,

And waits obſequious on the Queen's commands.

         To

To whom GOLFINIA: Fate-fulfilling maid,

Hear the Fates will, and be their will obey'd: 40

Straight to the field of fight thyself convey,

Where brave *Castalio* and *Pygmalion* stray;

There bid the long protracted combat cease,

And with thy bays *Castalio*'s temples grace.

She said; and swift, as *Hermes* from above 45

Shoots to perform the high behests of JOVE,

VICTORIA from her sister's presence flies,

Pleas'd to bestow the long disputed prize.

Mean while the Chiefs for the last hole contend,

The last great hole, which should their labours end;

For this the Chiefs exert their skill and might, 51

To drive the balls, and to direct their flight.

Thus two fleet coursers for the Royal plate,

(The others distanc'd,) run the final heat;

With all his might each gen'rous racer flies, 55

And all his art each panting rider tries,

While show'rs of gold and praises warm his breast,

And gen'rous emulation fires the beast.

C   His

His trufty club *Pygmalion* dauntlefs plies;

The ball ambitious climbs the lofty fkies; 60

But foon, ah! foon defcends upon the field;

The adverfe winds the lab'ring orb repell'd.

Thus when a fowl, whom wand'ring fportfmen fcare,

Leaves the fown land, and mounts the fields of air;

Short is his flight; the fiery *Furies* wound, 65

And bring him tumbling headlong to the ground.

 Not fo *Caftalio* lifts th'unerring club,

But with fuperior art attacks the globe;

The well-ftruck ball the ftormy wind beguil'd,

And like a fwallow fkim'd along the field. 70

 An harmlefs fheep, by Fate decreed to fall,

Feels the dire fury of the rapid ball;

Full on her front the raging bullet flew,

And fudden anguifh feiz'd the filent ew;

Stagg'ring fhe falls upon the verdant plain, 75

Convulfive pangs diftract her wounded brain.

Great PAN beheld her ftretch'd upon the grafs,

Nor unreveng'd permits the crime to pafs:

        Th' *Ar-*

Th' *Arcadian* God, with grief and fury ftung,

Snatch'd his ftout crook, and fierce to vengeance

   fprung,   80

His faithful dogs their mafter's fteps purfue,

The fleecy flocks before their father bow,

With bleatings hoarfe falute him as he ftrode,

And frifking lambkins dance around the God.

The Sire of Sheep then lifted from the ground 85

The panting dam, and pifs'd upon the wound:

The ftream divine foon eas'd the mother's pain;

The wife immortals never pifs in vain:

Then to the ball his horny foot applies;

Before his foot the kick'd offender flies; 90

The haplefs orb a gaping face detain'd,

Deep funk in fand the haplefs orb remain'd.

As VERDURILLA mark'd the ball's arreft,

She with refentment fir'd *Caftalio*'s breaft:

The nymph affum'd *Patrico*'s fhape and mien, 95

Like great *Patrico* ftalk'd along the green;

So well his manner and his accent feign'd,

Caftalio deem'd *Patrico*'s felf complain'd.

Ah fad difgrace! fee ruftic herds invade

GOLFINIAN plains, the angry Fairy faid. 100

Your ball abus'd, your hopes and projects croft,

The game endanger'd, and the hole nigh loft :

Thus brutal PAN refents his wounded ew,

Tho' Chance, not you, did guide the fatal blow.

Incens'd *Caftalio* makes her no replies, 105

T' attack the God, the furious mortal flies ;

His iron-headed club around he fwings,

And fierce at PAN the pond'rous weapon flings.

Affrighted PAN the dreadful miffive fhunn'd ;

But blamelefs *Tray* receiv'd a deadly wound : 110

Ill-fated *Tray* no more the flocks fhall tend,

In anguifh doom'd his fhorten'd life to end.

Nor could great PAN afford a timely aid ;

Great PAN himfelf before the hero fled :

Ev'n he a God a mortal's fury dreads, 115

And far and faft from bold *Caftalio* fpeeds.

           To

To free the ball the Chief now turns his mind,
Flies to the bank where lay the orb confin'd;
The pond'rous club upon the ball defcends,
Involv'd in duft th' exulting orb afcends;   120
Their loud applaufe the pleas'd fpectators raife,
The hollow bank refounds *Caftalio*'s praife.

A mighty blow *Pygmalion* then lets fall;
Straight from th' impulfive engine ftarts the ball,
Anfw'ring its mafter's juft defign, it haftes,   125
And from the hole fcarce twice two clubs length refts.

Ah! what avails thy fkill, fince Fate decrees
Thy conqu'ring foe to bear away the prize?

Full fifteen clubs length from the hole he lay,
A wide cart-road before him crofs'd his way;   130
The deep-cut tracks th' intrepid Chief defies,
High o'er the road the ball triumphing flies,
Lights on the green, and fcours into the hole:
Down with it finks deprefs'd *Pygmalion*'s foul.
Seiz'd with furprize th' affrighted hero ftands,   135
And feebly tips the ball with trembling hands;

The

The creeping ball its want of force complains,
A grassy tuft the loit'ring orb detains:
Surrounding crowds the victor's praise proclaim,
The ecchoing shore resounds *Castalio*'s name.   140

    For him *Pygmalion* must the bowl prepare,
To him must yield the honours of the war,
On Fame's triumphant wings his name shall soar,
Till time shall end, or GOFFING be no more.

F I N I S.

1763

THE
GOFF.

AN

Heroi - Comical Poem.

IN

THREE CANTOS.

✠✠✠✠✠✠✠✠✠✠✠✠✠✠✠✠✠✠✠✠✠✠✠✠✠✠✠✠✠✠✠✠✠✠

Cætera, quæ vacuas tenuiſſent carmina mentes,
Omnia jam volgata.   VIRG.

✠✠✠✠✠✠✠✠✠✠✠✠✠✠✠✠✠✠✠✠✠✠✠✠✠✠✠✠✠✠✠✠✠✠

The Second EDITION.

✠✠✠✠✠✠✠✠✠✠✠✠✠✠✠✠✠✠✠✠✠✠✠✠✠✠✠✠✠✠✠✠✠✠

EDINBURGH:

Printed for JAMES REID, Bookſeller in *Leith.*
M. DCC. LXIII.   (Price Four-pence)

✠✠✠✠✠✠✠✠✠✠✠✠✠✠✠✠✠✠✠✠✠✠✠✠✠

THE
GOFF.

CANTO I.

GOFF, and the *Man*, I sing, who, em'lous,
        plies
The jointed club; whose balls invade the
        skies;
Who from *Edina's* tow'rs, his peaceful home,
In quest of fame o'er *Letha's* plains did roam.
Long toil'd the hero, on the verdant field,   5
Strain'd his stout arm the weighty club to wield;
Such toils it cost, such labours to obtain
The bays of conquest, and the bowl to gain.

A 2   O thou

O, thou GOLFINIA, Goddess of these plains,

Great patroness of GOFF, indulge my strains; 10

Whether beneath the *thorn-tree* shade you lie,

Or from *Mercerian* tow'rs the game survey,

Or round the green the flying ball you chace

Or make your bed in some hot sandy *face:*

Leave your much lov'd abode, inspire his lays   15

Who sings of GOFF, and sings thy fav'rite's praise.

North from *Edina* eight furlongs and more

Lies that fam'd field, on *Fortha*'s founding shore.

Here, *Caledonian* Chiefs for health resort,

Confirm their sinews by the manly sport.   20

Macd――d and unmatch'd D――ple ply

Their pond'rous weapons, and the green defy;

R―tt―y for skill, and C――se for strength renown'd,

St――rt and L――sly beat the sandy ground,

And Br――n and Alst――n, Chiefs well known to fame,

And numbers more the Muse forbears to name.   26

Gigantic B――gg――r here full oft is seen,

Like huge Behemoth on an *Indian* green;

His

His bulk enormous fcarce can 'fcape the eyes,
Amaz'd fpectators wonder how he plies.. 30
Yea here great F——s, patron of the juft,
The dread of villains, and the good man's truft,
When fpent with toils in ferving human kind,
His body recreates, and unbends his mind.

Bright *Phœbus* now had meafur'd half the day 35
And warm'd the earth with genial noon-tide ray ;
Forth rufh'd *Caftalio* and his daring foe,
Both arm'd with clubs, and eager for the blow.
Of fineft afh *Caftalio*'s fhaft was made,
Pond'rous with lead, and fenc'd with horn the head,
(The work of *Dickfon*, who in *Letha* dwells, 41
And in the art of making clubs excels),
Which late beneath great *Claro*'s arm did bend,
But now is wielded by his greater friend.

Not with more fury *Norris* cleav'd the main, 45
To pour his thund'ring arms on guilty *Spain*;
Nor with more hafte brave *Haddock* bent his courfe,
To guard *Minorca* from *Iberian* force;

Than

Than thou, intrepid hero, urg'd thy way,
O'er roads and sands, impatient for the fray. 50

With equal warmth *Pygmalion* faft purfu'd,
(With courage oft are little wights endow'd)
'Till to GOLFINIA's downs the heroes came,
The fcene of combat, and the field of fame.

Upon a verdant bank, by FLORA grac'd, 55
Two fifter Fairies found the Goddefs plac'd;
Propp'd by her fnowy hand her head reclin'd,
Her curling locks hung waving in the wind.
She eyes intent the confecrated green,
Crowded with waving clubs, and vot'ries keen, 60
And hears the prayers of youths to her addrefs'd,
And from the hollow face relieves the ball diftrefs'd.
On either fide the fprightly Dryads fat,
And entertain'd the Goddefs with their chat.

First VERDURILLA, thus: O rural Queen! 65
What Chiefs are thofe that drive along the green?
With brandifh'd clubs the mighty heroes threat,
Their eager looks foretell a keen debate.

To

To whom GOLFINIA: Nymph, your eyes behold
Pygmalion ſtout, *Caſtalio* brave and bold.   70
From ſilver *Ierna*'s banks *Caſtalio* came,
But firſt on *Andrean* plains he courted fame.
His ſire, a Druid, taught (one day of ſeven)
The paths of virtue, the ſure road to heaven.
In *Pictiſh* capital the good man paſt   75 *Abernethy*
His virtuous life, and there he breath'd his laſt.
The ſon now dwells in fair *Edina*'s town,
And on our ſandy plains purſues renown.
See low *Pygmalion*, ſkill'd in GOFFING art,
Small is his ſize, but dauntleſs is his heart :   80
Faſt by a deſk in *Edin*'s domes he ſits,
With *ſaids* and *ſicklikes* length'ning out the writs.
For no mean prize the rival Chiefs contend,
But full rewards the victor's toils attend.
The vanquiſh'd hero for the victor fills,   85
A mighty bowl containing thirty gills ;
With nobleſt liquor is the bowl replete ;
Here ſweets and acids, ſtrength and weakneſs meet.

From

From *Indian* isles the strength and sweetness flow,
And *Tagus* banks their golden fruits bestow,   90
Cold *Caledonia*'s lucid streams controul
The fiery spirits, and fulfil the bowl.
For *Albion*'s peace and *Albion*'s friends they pray,
And drown in *punch* the labours of the day.

 The Goddess spoke, and thus GAMBOLIA pray'd;
Permit to join in brave *Pygmalion*'s aid,   96
O'er each deep road the hero to sustain,
And guide his ball to the desired plain.

 To this the Goddess of the manly sport:
Go, and be thou that daring Chief's support: 100
Let VERDURILLA be *Castalio*'s stay:
I from this flow'ry seat will view the fray.
She said: the nymphs trip nimbly o'er the green,
And to the combatants approach unseen.

The End of the first Canto.

CAN-

CANTO II.

YE rural powers that on these plains preside,
    Ye nymphs that dance on *Fortha*'s flow'ry side,
Assist the Muse that in your fields delights,
And guide her course in these uncommon flights.
But chief, thee, O GOLFINIA! I implore ;   5
High as thy balls instruct my Muse to soar :
So may thy green forever crowded be,
And balls on balls invade the azure sky.

    Now at that hole the Chiefs begin the game,
Which from the neighb'ring *thorn-tree* takes its name ;
Ardent they grasp the ball-compelling clubs,   11
And stretch their arms t'attack the little globes.
Not as our warriors brandish'd dreadful arms,
When fierce *Bellona* sounded war's alarms,
When conqu'ring *Cromwel* stain'd fair *Eska*'s flood 15
And soak'd her banks with *Caledonian* blood ;
Or when our bold ancestors madly fought,
And Clans engag'd for trifles or for nought.

That

That *Fury* now from our bless'd fields is driv'n,

To scourge unhappy nations doom'd by heav'n. 20

Let *Kouli Kan* destroy the fertile East,

Victorious *Vernon* thunder in the West;

Let horrid war involve perfidious *Spain*,

And GEORGE assert his empire o'er the main:

But on our plains *Britannia*'s sons engage, 25

And void of ire the sportive war they wage.

Lo, tatter'd *Irus*, who their armour bears,

Upon the green two little pyr'mids rears;

On these they place two balls with careful eye,

That with *Clarinda*'s breasts for colour vye, 30

The work of *Bobson*; who with matchless art

Shapes the firm hide, connecting ev'ry part,

Then in a socket sets the well-stitch'd void,

And thro' the eylet drives the downy tide;

Crowds urging crowds the forceful brogue impels, 35

The feathers harden and the leather swells;

He crams and sweats, yet crams and urges more,

Till scarce the turgid globe contains its store:

The

The dreadful falcon's pride here blended lies
With pigeons glossy down of various dyes; 40
The lark's small pinions join the common stock,
And yellow glory of the martial cock.

Soon as *Hyperion* gilds old *Andrea*'s spires,
From bed the artist to his cell retires;
With bended back, there plies his steely awls, 45
And shapes, and stuffs, and finishes the balls:
But when the glorious God of day has driv'n
His flaming chariot down the steep of heav'n,
He ends his labour, and with rural strains
Enchants the lovely maids and weary swains : 50
As thro' the streets the blythsome piper plays,
In antick dance they answer to his lays ;
At ev'ry pause the ravish'd crowd acclaim,
And rends the skies with tuneful *Bobson*'s name.
Not more rewarded was old *Amphion*'s song ; 55
That rear'd a town, and this drags one along.
Such is fam'd *Bobson*, who in *Andrea* thrives,
And such the balls each vig'rous hero drives.

First,

First, bold *Castalio*, ere he struck the blow,
Lean'd on his club, and thus address'd his foe :   60
Dares weak *Pygmalion* this stout arm defy,
Which brave *Matthias* doth with terror try?
Strong as he is, *Moravio* owns my might,
Distrusts his vigour, and declines the fight.
Renown'd *Clephanio* I constrain'd to yield,   65
And drove the haughty vet'ran from the field.
Weak is thine arm, rash youth, thy courage vain ;
Vanquish'd, with shame you'll curse the fatal plain.
The half-struck balls your weak endeavours mock,
Slowly proceed, and soon forget the stroke.   70
Not so the orb eludes my thund'ring force :
Thro' fields of air it holds its rapid course,
Swift as the balls from martial engines driv'n,
Streams like a comet thro' the arch of heav'n.

Vaunter, go on, (*Pygmalion* thus replies) ;   75
Thine empty boasts with justice I despise.
Hadst thou the strength *Goliah*'s spear to wield,
Like its great master thunder on the field,

And

And with that strength $C^{u\_}ll\_{}^{o}d\_{}^{e}n$'s matchless art,

Not one unmanly thought should daunt my heart. 80

He said, and sign'd to *Irus* ; who before,

With frequent warnings fill'd the sounding shore.

Then great *Castalio* his whole force collects,

And on the orb a noble blow directs.

Swift as a thought the ball obedient flies, 85

Sings high in air, and seems to cleave the skies ;

Then on the level plain its fury spends ;

And *Irus* to the Chief the welcome tidings sends.

Next in his turn *Pygmalion* strikes the globe :

On the upper half descends the erring club ; 90

Along the green the ball confounded scours ;

No lofty flight the ill-sped stroke impow'rs.

Thus, when the trembling hare descries the hounds,

She from her whinny mansion swiftly bounds ;

O'er hills and fields she scours, outstrips the wind ; 95

The hounds and huntsmen follow far behind.

GAMBOLIA now afforded timely aid ;

She o'er the sand the fainting ball convey'd,

Re-

Renew'd its force, and urg'd it on its way,
Till on the summit of the hill it lay.　100

Now all on fire the Chiefs their orbs pursue,
With the next stroke the orbs their flight renew;
Thrice round the green they urge the whizzing ball,
And thrice three holes to great *Castalio* fall;
The other six *Pygmalion* bore away,　105
And sav'd a while the honours of the day.

Had some brave champion of the sandy field
The Chiefs attended, and the game beheld;
With ev'ry stroke his wonder had increaft,
And em'lous fires had kindled in his breaft.　110

The End of the second Canto.

C A N-

CANTO III.

HArmonious Nine, that from *Parnassus* view
The subject world, and all that's done below;
Who from oblivion snatch the patriot's name,
And to the stars extol the hero's fame,
Bring each your lyre, and to my song repair,   5
Nor think GOLFINIA's train below the Muses care.

Declining *Sol* with milder beams invades
The *Scotian* fields, and lengthens out the shades;
Hastes to survey the conquer'd golden plains,
Where captive *Indians* mourn in *Spanish* chains;   10
To gild the waves where hapless *Hosier* dy'd,
Where *Vernon* late proud *Bourbon*'s force defy'd,
Triumphant rode along the wat'ry plain,
Britannia's glory and the scourge of *Spain*.

Still from her seat the *Power* of GOFF beheld
Th' unweary'd heroes toiling on the field: 16
The light-foot Fairies in their labours share,
Each nymph her hero seconds in the war;

Pyg-

Pygmalion and GAMBOLIA there appear,

And VERDURILLA with *Castalio* here.　　　　20

The Goddeſs ſaw, and op'd the book of Fate,

To ſearch the iſſue of the grand debate.

Bright ſilver plates the ſacred leaves infold,

Bound with twelve ſhining claſps of ſolid gold.

The wond'rous book contains the fate of all　　25

That lift the club, and ſtrike the miſſive ball;

Myſterious rhymes that thro' the pages flow,

The paſt, the preſent, and the future ſhow.

GOLFINIA reads the Fate-foretelling lines,

And ſoon the ſequel of the war divines;　　　30

Sees conqueſt doom'd *Castalio*'s toils to crown,

Pygmalion doom'd ſuperior might to own.

Then at her ſide VICTORIA ſtraight appears,

Her ſiſter Goddeſs, arbitreſs of wars.

Upon her head a wreath of bays ſhe wore,　　35

And in her hand a laurel ſceptre bore;

Anxious to know the will of Fate ſhe ſtands,

And waits obſequious on the Queen's commands.

　　　　　　　　　　　　　　　　　To

To whom GOLFINIA: Fate-fulfilling maid,
Hear the Fates will, and be their will obey'd: 43
Straight to the field of fight thyself convey,
Where brave *Castalio* and *Pygmalion* stray;
There bid the long protracted combat cease,
And with thy bays *Castalio*'s temples grace.
She said; and swift, as *Hermes* from above   45
Shoots to perform the high behests of JOVE,
VICTORIA from her sister's presence flies,
Pleas'd to bestow the long disputed prize.

Mean while the Chiefs for the last hole contend,
The last great hole, which should their labours end;
For this the Chiefs exert their skill and might,   51
To drive the balls, and to direct their flight.
Thus two fleet coursers for the Royal plate,
(The others distanc'd,) run the final heat;
With all his might each gen'rous racer flies,   55
And all his art each panting rider tries,
While show'rs of gold and praises warm his breast,
And gen'rous emulation fires the beast.

C

His

His trusty club *Pygmalion* dauntless plies;
The ball ambitious climbs the lofty skies; 60
But soon, ah! soon descends upon the field;
The adverse winds the lab'ring orb repell'd.
Thus when a fowl, whom wand'ring sportsmen scare,
Leaves the sown land, and mounts the fields of air,
Short is his flight; the fiery *Furies* wound, 65
And bring him tumbling headlong to the ground.

Not so *Castalio* lifts th'unerring club,
But with superior art attacks the globe;
The well-struck ball the stormy wind beguil'd,
And like a swallow skim'd along the field. 70
An harmless sheep, by Fate decreed to fall.
Feels the dire fury of the rapid ball;
Full on her front the raging bullet flew,
And sudden anguish seiz'd the silent ew;
Stagg'ring she falls upon the verdant plain, 75
Convulsive pangs distract her wounded brain.
Great PAN beheld her stretch'd upon the grass,
Nor unreveng'd permits the crime to pass;

C   Th' *Ar-*

Th' *Arcadian* God, with grief and fury stung,

Snatch'd his stout crook, and fierce to vengeance

    sprung,   81

His faithful dogs their master's steps pursue;

The fleecy flocks before their father bow,

With bleatings hoarse salute him as he strode,

And frisking lambkins dance around the God.   85

The fire of sheep then lifted from the ground,

The panting dam, and pifs'd upon the wound:

The stream divine soon eas'd the mother's pain;

The wise immortals never pifs in vain:

Then to the ball his horny foot applies;

Before his foot the kick'd offender flies;   90

The haplefs orb a gaping face detain'd,

Deep sunk in sand the haplefs orb remain'd.

    As VERDURILLA mark'd the ball's arrest,

She with resentment fir'd *Castalio's* breast:

The nymph assum'd *Patrico's* shape and mien,   95

Like great *Patrico* stalk'd along the green;

So well his manner and his accent feign'd,
Castalio deem'd *Patrico*'s self complain'd.
Ah sad disgrace! see rustic herds invade
GOLFINIAN plains; the angry Fairy said.   100
Your ball abus'd, your hopes and projects croft,
The game endanger'd, and the hole nigh loft:
Thus brutal PAN resents his wounded ew,
Tho' chance, not you, did guide the fatal blow.

Incens'd *Castalio* makes her no replies,   105
T' attack the God, the furious mortal flies;
His iron-headed club around he swings,
And fierce at PAN the pond'rous weapon flings.
Affrighted PAN the dreadful missive shunn'd;
But blameless *Tray* receiv'd a deadly wound: 110
Ill-fated *Tray* no more the flocks shall tend,
In anguish doom'd his shorten'd life to end.
Nor could great PAN afford a timely aid;
Great PAN himself before the hero fled:
Even he a God a mortal's fury dreads,   115
And far and fast from bold *Castalio* speeds.

To

To free the ball the Chief now turns his mind,
Flies to the bank where lay the orb confin'd;
The pond'rous club upon the ball descends,
Involv'd in dust th' exulting orb ascends ; 120
Their loud applause the pleas'd spectators raise,
The hollow bank resounds *Castalio*'s praise.

A mighty blow *Pygmalion* then lets fall;
Straight from th' impulsive engine starts the ball,
Answ'ring its master's just design, it hastes, 125
And from the hole scarce twice two clubs length rests.

Ah ! what avails thy skill, since Fate decrees
Thy conqu'ring foe to bear away the prize?

Full fifteen clubs length from the hole he lay,
A wide cart-road before him cross'd his way ; 130
The deep-cut tracks th' intrepid Chief defies,
High o'er the road the ball triumphing flies,
Lights on the green, and scours into the hole :
Down with it sinks depress'd *Pygmalion*'s soul.
Seiz'd with surprize th' affrighted hero stands ; 135
And feebly tips the ball with trembling hands ;

The

The creeping ball its want of force complains,
A grassy tuft, the loit'ring orb detains:
Surrounding crowds the victor's praise proclaim,
The ecchoing shore resounds *Castalio*'s name. 140

For him *Pygmalion* must the bowl prepare,
To him must yield the honours of the war,
On Fame's triumphant wings his name shall soar,
Till time shall end, or GOFFING be no more.

FINIS.

BOOKS, PLAYS, POEMS, *&c.*
SOLD BY
JAMES REID, Bookseller in LEITH.

ABelard and Heloisa, in verse and prose.	Ambitious Step-mother
	Armstrongon health, a poem.
Account of the ancient alliance betwixt the Scots and French.	Artful husband.
	Assembly.
Albion queens.	All's well that ends well.
Author.	Barbarossa.
Alchemist.	Beaux Stratagem.
Amphytrion.	Busy Body.
All for love.	Beggars opera.
All in the wrong.	Busireis.
Alzira.	Blind beggar.
Amorous widow.	Boarding School.
Anna Bullen.	Bold stroke for a wife.
Alfred.	Brave Irishman.
Apprentice.	Brothers.

Ceius

Caius Marius.
Cleone.
Careless husband.
Chaplet.
Cato.
Country wife.
Characters of Theophrastus.
Chrononhotonthologos.
Cobler of preston.
Comus.
Country lasses
Conscious lovers.
Constant couple.
Coriolanus.
Cymbeline.
Country wit.
Damon and Phillida.
Devil to pay.
Devil of a wife.
Dispensary, a poem.
Distressed mother.
Don Sebastian.
Double dealer.
Double Gallant.
Douglas.
Dragon of Wantley.
Drummer.
Duke of Guise.
Æsop.
Eurydice.
Earl of Essex.
Elfrida.
Earl of Haddington's poems.
Englishman in Paris.
Every man in his humour.
Fair Circassian.
Evening love.
Fair penitent.
Fair quaker of Deal.
False Friend.
Fond husband.
Fatal marriage.
Flora or Hob in the well.
Foundling.   [nion
Free mason's pocket compa-
Funeral.
Frenchman in London.

Gentle shepherd.
Gustavus Vasa.
George Barnwell.
Greenwich Park.
Hamlet.
Humours of Oxford.
Hammond's love-elegies.
Henry IV. two parts.
High life below stairs.
Honest Yorkshire-man.
Hospital for fools.
Heroic Daughter.
Humorous Lieutenant.
Jane Gray.
Jovial Crew.
Jane Shore.
Jealous Wife.
Inconstant.
Indian emperor.
Intriguing chambermaid.
Julius Cæsar.
King Henry V.
King Lear.
King Henry III.
King Richard III.
King Arthur.
Lethe.
Lottery.
Love alamode.
Love for love.
Love in a wood.
Love in a tub.
Lying lover.
Love makes a man.
Love's last shift.
Love in a bottle.
Lying valet.
Ladies last stake.
Love in a village.
Macbeath.
Man of mode.
Mariamne.
Marriage ala mode.
Merope.
Musical Lady.
Merry wives of Windsor.
Miller of Mansfield.

Mira-

Miraculous escape of the young
  Chevalier, with a large ac-
  count of what befel him in
  France.
Miser.
Modern wife.
Miss in her teens.
Mock doctor.
Merchant of Venice.
Mourning bride.
Oeconomy of human life.
Oeconomy of love.
Oracle.
Oroonoko.
Orphan.
Othello.
Oedipus.
Pennecuik's poems.
Perjured husband.
Phædra and Hypolitus.
Poem on the grave.
Polite philosopher.
Pope's essay on man.
——moral essays.
——rape of the lock.
Present for an apprentice.
Provoked husband.
Provoked wife.
Recruiting officer.
Rehearsal.
Reid's Scots gardiner, for the
  climate of Scotland.
Reprisal.
Register office.
Revenge.
Roman Father,
Rival queens.
Relapse.
Romeo and Juliet.
Royal convert.
Rule a wife and have a wife.
Shepherd of Banbury.
She would and she would not.

She would if she could.
Siege of Damascus.
Sir Hary Wildair.
Sir Courtly Nice.
Spanish friar.
Sir Martin Marrall.
Stage coach.
Soldiers fortune.
State of innocence.
Suspicious husband.
Tamerlane.
Tancred and Sigismunda.
Tempest.
Tender husband.
The guardian.
The knights.
The splendid shilling.
Timon of Athens.
Tom Thumb.
Toy-shop.
Trick for trick.
True-born Englishman.
Tunbridge walks.
Ulysses.
Universal gallant.
Upholsterer.
Venice preserved.
Village opera.
Virgin unmasked.
Volpone.
Wife's relief.
Way of the world.
Way to keep him.
Wife to be let.
Wild gallant.
Wonder, a woman keeps a se-
  cret.
Woman's a riddle.
Wooden world, or the cha-
  racter of a ship of war.
Woman's revenge.
Zara.

1793

THE

GOFF.

AN

HEROI-COMICAL POEM.

IN

THREE CANTOS.

SECOND EDITION. *(this is the 3rd edition)*

WITH AN

APPENDIX,

CONTAINING

TWO POEMS IN PRAISE OF GOFF, AND A FEW
NOTES AND ILLUSTRATIONS.

*Caetera, quae vacuas tenuiſſent carmina mentes,
Omnia jam volgata.*——VIRG.

EDINBURGH:
PRINTED FOR PETER HILL.
1793.

TO

ALL THE LOVERS

OF

G O F F,

IN EUROPE, ASIA, AFRICA, AND AMERICA,

THE FOLLOWING POEM

IS MOST HUMBLY INSCRIBED

BY

THE PUBLISHER.

THE following beautiful Poem, first printed in Edinburgh in 1743, was written by Mr THOMAS MATHISON, then a Writer, or Agent, in Edinburgh. After he quitted that employment, he went into holy orders as a Clergyman: His first charge was a Presbyterian Congregation in the north of England. His piety and extensive usefulness rendered him the object of the high veneration of his parishioners, and of all those who had the happiness of his acquaintance. Having continued there for some years, he was afterwards, by the interest of President Forbes, appointed Minister in Brechin, where he died in 1754.

The EDITOR acknowledges his obligations to a friend for the use of a copy of this Poem, by which he has been enabled to supply the names of the most celebrated Goffers left blank in the First Edition: He likewise offers his grateful thanks to the Gentlemen who have enriched this small piece with two excellent Songs in praise of Goff.

THE

THE game of Goff has been known and practised in Scotland upwards of four hundred years.

It is pleafant to remark, that Goff, originally a Scotch game, has been introduced, not only into England and Ireland, but almoft into every other country in Europe: It has found its way into the Weft, nor is it unknown in the Eaft, Indies; America, too, boafts of her fkill in the art of Goffing.

At prefent there are many Goffing Societies in Scotland, and in our fifter kingdoms. Their principal object is to promote the practice of this manly exercife, which, befides amufement and recreation, greatly contributes to reftore and preferve the health of body and mind.

THE

THE

G O F F.

CANTO I.

Goff, and the *Man*, I sing, who, em'lous plies
The jointed club, whose balls invade the skies,
Who from *Edina's* tow'rs, his peaceful home,
In quest of fame o'er *Letha's* plains did roam.
Long toil'd the hero on the verdant field,   5
Strain'd his stout arm the weighty club to wield;
Such toils it cost, such labours to obtain
The bays of conquest, and the bowl to gain.

A   O

O thou, GOLFINIA, Goddess of these plains,
Great patroness of GOFF, indulge my strains;   10.
Whether beneath the *thorn-tree* shade you lie,
Or from *Mercerian* tow'rs the game survey,
Or 'round the green the flying ball you chase,
Or make your bed in some hot sandy *face* :
Leave your much lov'd abode, inspire his lays   15
Who sings of GOFF, and sings thy fav'rite's praise.

 North from *Edina* eight furlongs and more
Lies that fam'd field, on *Fortha's* founding shore.
Here, *Caledonian* Chiefs for health resort,
Confirm their sinews by the manly sport.   20
Macdonald, and unmatch'd *Dalrymple* ply
Their pond'rous weapons, and the green defy;
Rattray for skill, and *Corse* for strength renown'd,
Stewart and *Lesly* beat the sandy ground,
And *Brown* and *Alston*, Chiefs well known to fame,   25
And numbers more the Muse forbears to name.
Gigantic *Biggar* here full oft is seen,
Like huge Behemoth on an *Indian* green;

            His

His bulk enormous fcarce can 'fcape the eyes,

Amaz'd fpectators wonder how he plies.   30

Yea here great *Forbes*, patron of the juft,

The dread of villains, and the good man's truft,

When fpent with toils in ferving human kind,

His body recreates, and unbends his mind.

Bright *Phoebus*, now, had meafur'd half the day,   35

And warm'd the earth with genial noontide ray:

Forth rufh'd *Caftalio* and his daring foe,

Both arm'd with clubs, and eager for the blow.

Of fineft afh *Caftalio's* fhaft was made,

Pond'rous with lead, and fenc'd with horn the head,   40

(The work of *Dickfon*, who in *Letha* dwells,

And in the art of making clubs excels),

Which late beneath great *Claro's* arm did bend,

But now is wielded by his greater friend.

Not with more fury *Norris* cleav'd the main,   45

To pour his thund'ring arms on guilty *Spain*;

Nor

Nor with more hafte brave *Haddock* bent his courfe,

To guard *Minorca* from *Iberian* force :

Than thou, intrepid hero, urg'd thy way,

O'er roads and fands, impatient for the fray.　　50

With equal warmth *Pygmalion* faft purfu'd,

(With courage oft are little wights endow'd),

'Till to GOLFINIA's downs the heroes came,

The fcene of combat, and the field of fame.

Upon a verdant bank, by FLORA grac'd,　　55

Two fifter Fairies found the Goddefs plac'd ;

Prop'd by her fnowy hand her head reclin'd,

Her curling locks hung waving in the wind.

She eyes intent the confecrated green,

Crowded with waving clubs, and vot'ries keen,　　60

And hears the prayers of youths to her addrefs'd,

And from the hollow *face* relieves the ball diftrefs'd.

On either fide the fprightly Dryads fat,

And entertain'd the Goddefs with their chat.

First

First, VERDURILLA thus: O rural Queen!   65

What Chiefs are those that drive along the green?

With brandish'd clubs the mighty heroes threat,

Their eager looks foretel a keen debate.

To whom GOLFINIA: Nymph, your eyes behold

Pygmalion stout, *Castalio* brave and bold.   70

From silver *Ierna's* banks *Castalio* came,

But first on *Andrean* plains he courted fame.

His sire, a Druid, taught (one day of seven)

The paths of virtue, the sure road to heaven.

In *Pictish* capital the good man past   75

His virtuous life, and there he breath'd his last.

The son now dwells in fair *Edina's* town,

And on our sandy plains pursues renown.

See low *Pygmalion*, skill'd in GOFFING art,

Small is his size, but dauntless is his heart: 80

Fast by a desk in *Edin's* domes he sits,

With *saids* and *sicklikes* length'ning out the writs.

For no mean prize the rival Chiefs contend,

But full rewards the victor's toils attend.

         B   The

The vanquish'd hero for the victor fills

A mighty bowl containing thirty gills;

With noblest liquor is the bowl replete;

Here sweets and acids, strength and weakness meet.

From *Indian* isles the strength and sweetness flow,

And *Tagus'* banks their golden fruits bestow,   90

Cold *Caledonia's* lucid streams controul

The fiery spirits, and fulfil the bowl.

For *Albion's* peace and *Albion's* friends they pray,

And drown in *punch* the labours of the day.

The Goddess spoke, and thus GAMBOLIA pray'd: 95

Permit to join in brave *Pygmalion's* aid,

O'er each deep road the hero to sustain,

And guide his ball to the desired plain.

To this the Goddess of the manly sport:

Go, and be thou that daring Chief's support;   100

Let VERDURILLA be *Castalio's* stay;

I from this flow'ry seat will view the fray.

She

She said : The nymphs trip nimbly o'er the green,
And to the combatants approach unseen.

THE END OF THE FIRST CANTO.

CANTO

CANTO II.

YE rural powers that on thefe plains prefide,
Ye nymphs that dance on *Fortha's* flow'ry fide,
Affift the Mufe that in your fields delights,
And guide her courfe in thefe uncommon flights.
But chief, thee, O GOLFINIA ! I implore ;
High as thy balls inftruct my Mufe to foar :
So may thy green forever crowded be,
And balls on balls invade the azure fky.

Now at that hole the Chiefs begin the game,
Which from the neighb'ring *thorn-tree* takes its name ;   10
Ardent they grafp the ball-compelling clubs,
And ftretch their arms t'attack the little globes.
Not as our warriors brandifh'd dreadful arms,
When fierce *Bellona* founded wars alarms,

When

When conqu'ring *Cromwel* ftain'd fair *Eſka's* flood   15
And ſoak'd her banks with *Caledonian* blood ;
Or when our bold anceſtors madly fought,
And Clans engag'd for trifles or for nought.
That *Fury* now from our bleſs'd fields is driv'n,
To ſcourge unhappy nations doom'd by heav'n.   20
Let *Kouli Kan* deſtroy the fertile Eaſt,
Victorious *Vernon* thunder in the Weſt ;
Let horrid war involve perfidious *Spain,*
And GEORGE aſſert his empire o'er the Main :
But on our plains *Britannia's* ſons engage,   25
And void of ire the ſportive war they wage.

Lo, tatter'd *Irus,* who their armour bears,
Upon the green two little pyr'mids rears ;
On theſe they place two balls with careful eye,
That with *Clarinda's* breaſts for colour vie,   30
The work of *Bobſon ;* who with matchleſs art
Shapes the firm hide, connecting ev'ry part,
Then in a ſocket ſets the well-ſtitch'd void,
And thro' the eylet drives the downy tide ;

C   Crowds

Crowds urging crowds the forceful brogue impels,   35
The feathers harden and the Leather swells ;
He crams and sweats, yet crams and urges more;
Till scarce the turgid globe contains its store :
The dreadful falcon's pride here blended lies
With pigeons glossy down of various dyes ;   40
The lark's small pinions join the common stock,
And yellow glory of the martial cock.

Soon as *Hyperion* gilds o'er *Andrea's* spires,
From bed the artist to his cell retires ;
With bended back, there plies his steely awls,   45
And shapes, and stuffs, and finishes the balls.
But when the glorious God of day has driv'n
His flaming chariot down the steep of heav'n,
He ends his labour, and with rural strains
Enchants the lovely maids and weary swains :   50
As thro' the streets the blythsome piper plays,
In antick dance they answer to his lays ;
At ev'ry pause the ravish'd crowd acclaim,
And rend the skies with tuneful *Bobson's* name.

Not

Not more rewarded was old *Amphion*'s song ;   55
That rear'd a town, and this drags one along.
Such is fam'd *Bobfon*, who in *Andrea* thrives,
And such the balls each vig'rous hero drives.

 First, bold *Caftalio*, ere he ftruck the blow,
Lean'd on his club, and thus addrefs'd his foe :   60
Dares weak *Pygmalion* this ftout arm defy,
Which brave *Matthias* doth with terror try ?
Strong as he is, *Moravio* owns my might,
Diftrufts his vigour, and declines the fight.
Renown'd *Clephanio* I conftrain'd to yield,   65
And drove the haughty vet'ran from the field.
Weak is thine arm, rafh youth, thy courage vain ;
Vanquifh'd, with fhame you'll curfe the fatal plain.
The half-ftruck balls your weak endeavours mock,
Slowly proceed, and foon forget the ftroke.   70
Not fo the orb eludes my thund'ring force ;
Thro' fields of air it holds its rapid courfe,

          Swift

Swift as the balls from martial engines driv'n,
Streams like a comet thro' the arch of heav'n.

Vaunter, go on, (*Pygmalion* thus replies) ;   75
Thine empty boasts with justice I despise.
Hadst thou the strength *Goliah's* spear to wield,
Like its great master thunder on the field,
And with that strength *C-ll-d-n's* matchless art,
Not one unmanly thought should daunt my heart. 80
He said, and sign'd to *Irus* ; who, before,
With frequent warnings fill'd the sounding shore.

Then great *Castalio* his whole force collects,
And on the orb a noble blow directs.
Swift as a thought the ball obedient flies,   85
Sings high in air, and seems to cleave the skies ;
Then on the level plain its fury spends ;
And *Irus* to the Chief the welcome tidings sends.
Next in his turn *Pygmalion* strikes the globe :
On th' upper half descends the erring club ;   90

Along

Along the green the ball confounded fcours ;
No lofty flight the ill-fped ftroke impow'rs.

Thus, when the trembling hare defcries the hounds,
She from her whinny manfion fwiftly bounds ;
O'er hills and fields fhe fcours, outftrips the wind ;   95
The hounds and huntfmen follow far behind.

GAMBOLIA now afforded timely aid ;
She o'er the fand the fainting ball convey'd,
Renew'd its force, and urg'd it on its way,
Till on the fummit of the hill it lay.   100

Now all on fire the Chiefs their orbs purfue,
With the next ftroke the orbs their flight renew :
Thrice round the green they urge the whizzing ball,
And thrice three holes to great *Caftalio* fall ;
The other fix *Pygmalion* bore away,   105
And fav'd a while the honours of the day.

D   Had

Had some brave champion of the sandy field
The Chiefs attended, and the game beheld;
With ev'ry stroke his wonder had increast,
And em'lous fires had kindled in his breast.   110

THE END OF THE SECOND CANTO.

CANTO

CANTO III.

Harmonious Nine, that from *Parnassus* view
The subject world, and all that's done below;
Who from oblivion snatch the patriot's name,
And to the stars extol the hero's fame,
Bring each your lyre, and to my song repair,   5
Nor think GOLFINIA's train below the Muses care.

   Declining *Sol* with milder beams invades
The *Scotian* fields, and lengthens out the shades;
Hastes to survey the conquer'd golden plains,
Where captive *Indians* mourn in *Spanish* chains;   10
To gild the waves where hapless *Hosier* dy'd,
Where *Vernon* late proud *Bourbon's* force defy'd,
Triumphant rode along the wat'ry plain,
Britannia's glory, and the scourge of *Spain*.

                                      Still

Still from her feat the *Power* of GOFF beheld   15
Th' unweary'd heroes toiling on the field :
The light-foot *Fairies* in their labours fhare,
Each nymph her hero feconds in the war ;
Pygmalion and GAMBOLIA there appear,
And VERDURILLA with *Caftalio* here.   20
The Goddefs faw, and op'd the book of Fate,
To fearch the iffue of the grand debate.

Bright filver plates the facred leaves infold,
Bound with twelve fhining clafps of folid gold.
The wond'rous book contains the fate of all   25
That lift the club, and ftrike the miffive ball ;
Myfterious rhymes that thro' the pages flow,
The paft, the prefent, and the future fhow.
GOLFINIA reads the Fate-foretelling lines,
And foon the fequel of the war divines ;   30
Sees conqueft doom'd *Caftalio's* toils to crown,
Pygmalion doom'd fuperior might to own.
Then at her fide VICTORIA ftraight appears,
Her fifter Goddefs, arbitrefs of wars.

Upon

Upon her head a wreath of bays fhe wore,   35
And in her hand a laurel fceptre bore ;
Anxious to know the will of Fate fhe ftands,
And waits obfequious on the Queen's commands.

To whom GOLFINIA : Fate-fulfilling maid,
Hear the Fates will, and be their will obey'd :   40
Straight to the field of fight thyfelf convey,
Where brave *Caftalio* and *Pygmalion* ftray ;
There bid the long protracted combat ceafe,
And with thy bays *Caftalio's* temples grace.
She faid ; and fwift, as *Hermes* from above   45
Shoots to perform the high behefts of JOVE,
VICTORIA from her fifter's prefence flies,
Pleas'd to beftow the long difputed prize.

Meanwhile the Chiefs for the laft hole contend,
The laft great hole, which fhould their labours end ; 50
For this the Chiefs exert their fkill and might,
To drive the balls, and to direct their flight.

    E   Thus

Thus two fleet courfers for the Royal plate,
(The others diftanc'd), run the final heat ;
With all his might each gen'rous racer flies, 55
And all his art each panting rider tries,
While fhow'rs of gold and praifes warm his breaft,
And gen'rous emulation fires the beaft.

His trufty club *Pygmalion* dauntlefs plies ;
The ball ambitious climbs the lofty fkies ; 60
But foon, ah ! foon defcends upon the field ;
The adverfe winds the lab'ring orb repell'd.
Thus when a fowl, whom wand'ring fportfmen fcare,
Leaves the fowen land, and mounts the fields of air,
Short is his flight ; the fiery *Furies* wound, 65
And bring him tumbling headlong to the ground.

Not fo *Caftalio* lifts th' unerring club,
But with fuperior art attacks the globe ;
The well-ftruck ball the ftormy wind beguil'd,
And like a fwallow fkim'd along the field. 70

An

An harmlefs fheep, by Fate decreed to fall

Feels the dire fury of the rapid ball ;

Full on her front the raging bullet flew,

And fudden anguifh feiz'd the filent ewe ;

Stagg'ring fhe falls upon the verdant plain, 75

Convulfive pangs diftract her wounded brain.

Great PAN beheld her ftretch'd upon the grafs,

Nor unreveng'd permits the crime to pafs :

Th' *Arcadian* God, with grief and fury ftung,

Snatch'd his ftout crook, and fierce to vengeance fprung ; 80

His faithful dogs their mafter's fteps purfue,

The fleecy flocks before their father bow,

With bleatings hoarfe falute him as he ftrode,

And frifking lambkins dance around the God.

The Sire of Sheep then lifted from the ground 85

The panting dam, and pifs'd upon the wound :

The ftream divine foon eas'd the mother's pain ;

The wife immortals never pifs in vain :

Then to the ball his horny foot applies ;

Before his foot the kick'd offender flies ; 90

       The

The haplefs orb a gaping face detain'd,
Deep funk in fand the haplefs orb remain'd.

As VERDURILLA mark'd the ball's arreft,
She with refentment fir'd *Caftalio's* breaft:
The nymph affum'd *Patrico's* fhape and mien,   95
Like great *Patrico* ftalk'd along the green ;
So well his manner and his accent feign'd,
Caftalio deem'd *Patrico's* felf complain'd.
Ah fad difgrace ! fee ruftic herds invade
GOLFINIAN plains, the angry *Fairy* faid.   100
Your ball abus'd, your hopes and projects croft,
The game endanger'd, and the hole nigh loft :
Thus brutal PAN refents his wounded ewe,
Tho' Chance, not you, did guide the fatal blow.

Incens'd *Caftalio* makes her no replies,   105
T' attack the God, the furious mortal flies ;
His iron-headed club around he fwings,
And fierce at PAN the pond'rous weapon flings.

Affrighted

Affrighted PAN the dreadful miffive fhunn'd ;

But blamelefs *Tray* receiv'd a deadly wound :　　　110

Ill-fated *Tray* no more the flocks fhall tend,

In anguifh doom'd his fhorten'd life to end ;

Nor could great PAN afford a timely aid ;

Great PAN himfelf before the hero fled :

Ev'n he a God a mortal's fury dreads,　　　115

And far and faft from bold *Caftalio* fpeeds.

To free the ball the Chief now turns his mind,

Flies to the bank where lay the orb confin'd ;

The pond'rous club upon the ball defcends,

Involv'd in duft th' exulting orb afcends ;　　　120

Their loud applaufe the pleas'd fpectators raife,

The hollow bank refounds *Caftalio's* praife.

A mighty blow *Pygmalion* then lets fall ;

Straight from th' impulfive engine ftarts the ball,

Anfw'ring its mafter's juft defign, it haftes,　　　125

And from the hole fcarce twice two clubs lengths refts.

F　　　　　　　　　　　　　　　　Ah !

Ah! what avails thy fkill, fince Fate decrees
Thy conqu'ring foe to bear away the prize?

Full fifteen clubs length from the hole he lay,
A wide cart-road before him crofs'd his way ;   130
The deep-cut tracks th' intrepid Chief defies,
High o'er the road the ball triumphing flies,
Lights on the green, and fcours into the hole :
Down with it finks deprefs'd *Pygmalion's* foul.
Seiz'd with furprife th' affrighted hero ftands,   135
And feebly tips the ball with trembling hands ;
The creeping ball its want of force complains,
A graffy tuft the loit'ring orb detains :
Surrounding crowds the victor's praife proclaim,
The echoing fhore refounds *Caftalio's* name.   140

For him *Pygmalion* muft the bowl prepare,
To him muft yield the honours of the war ;
On Fame's triumphant wings his name fhall foar,
Till time fhall end, or GOFFING be no more.

APPENDIX.

APPENDIX.

SONG

IN PRAISE OF

GOFF.

TUNE.—" *Hey derry down*," &c.

I.

OF rural diversions too long has the Chace
All the honours usurp'd, and assum'd the chief place;
But truth bids the Muse from henceforward proclaim,
That GOFF, first of sports, shall stand foremost in fame.

II.

II.

At GOFF we contend without rancour or spleen,

And bloodless the laurels we reap on the green;

From vig'rous exertions our raptures arise,

And to crown our delights no poor fugitive dies.

III.

From exercise keen, from strength active and bold,

We'll traverse the green, and forget we are old:

Blue Devils, diseases, dull sorrow and care,

Knock'd down by our Balls as they whizz thro' the air.

IV.

The strong sinewed son of Alcmena wou'd drub,

And demolish a monster, when arm'd with a club;

But what were the monsters which Hercules slew,

To those fiends which each week with our Clubs we subdue?

V.

Health, harmony, happiness, friendship, and fame,

Are the fruits and rewards of our favourite game.

A

A spirit so distinguish'd the Fair must approve :

Then to GOFF give the day, and the ev'ning to love.

VI.

Then a bumper fill round, that each social soul

May drink to the *Putter*, the *Balls*, and the *Hole* ;

And thro' life may each Goffer invariably find

His opponent play fair, and his *Fair-one* prove kind.

VII.

O'er the Links, see our heroes in uniform clad,

In parties well match'd, how we orderly spread ;

While with long strokes and short strokes we tend to the goal,

And with *put* well directed *plump* into the *hole*.

G   THE

THE

GOFFERS.

Tune.—" *Fy gar rub.*"

I.

WHILE round the Links our Balls we play,
What tho' with *rubs* we sometimes meet,
We still *push* on, all brisk and gay,
Such *chances* make the game more sweet :
So 'tis in playing life's great game ;
Variety's the source of joy ;
If each day's *course* was just the same,
The tedious *circle* soon would cloy.

II.

II.

And thus, my friends, while here we fit,
We each by various methods ftrive
To banifh care, *ftrike ftrokes* of wit,
And far around us mirth to *drive :*
One tells the tale with merry glee,
Another fings the chearful fong,
His pow'rs each clubs, whate'er they be,
The *match* of pleafure to prolong.

III.

So may we ftill, with manly fport,
Our nerves well brace upon the green,
Then to the focial board refort,
Where playful mirth is always feen :
And as the hours fly fwiftly on,
May we their *well-mark'd* pleafures feize ;
Thus fhall the *game* of life be *won*,
And we play out the *round* with eafe.

NOTES

NOTES AND ILLUSTRATIONS

TO THE

POEM

ON

GOFF.

CANTO I.

Line 31.—*Forbes :* Duncan Forbes, Efq; Lord Prefident of the Court of Seffion in Scotland. It is reported of this great man, that he was fo fond of Goff, as to play on the Sands of Leith when the Links were covered with fnow.

Line 37.—*Caftalio :* Mr Alexander Dunning, late governor of Watfon's Hofpital ; an excellent claffical fcholar.

Line 41.—For *Dickfon,* read *Neilfon.*

> The work of Neilfon, whofe fuperior fkill,
>
> Tho' often rival'd, yet unequal'd ftill.

Line 45.—*Norris :* The brave Admiral Norris.

H

Line

Line 47.—*Haddock :* The intrepid Admiral of that name.

Line 49.—Than thou, intrepid hero, urg'd thy way,

        Than bold *Caſtalio* urgent puſh'd his way.

Line 51.—*Pygmalion :* The ingenious Mr THOMAS MATHISON, author of the Poem.

See the Introduction; ſee alſo line 79. 80. 81. 82. and 83. of the Poem, where

he deſcribes his low ſtature, his ſkill in Goffing, and his employment at the deſk,

as a writer.

Line 62.—And from the hollow face relieves the ball diſtreſs'd,—dele *hollow*.

Line 67.—With brandiſh'd clubs, &c.

        Their poliſh'd clubs the mighty heroes raiſe,

        And each anticipates the victor's praiſe.

CANTO II.

Line 1.———that *on* theſe plains preſide,

        ———that *o'er* theſe plains preſide.

Line 10.———*thorn-tree* takes its name.—A little to the ſouth of the hole where

the Goffers now ſtrike off their firſt ball, formerly grew a venerable thorn ;

hence it is called at this day *The Thorn-tree Hole*.

Line 17.———bold anceſtors madly fought,

        ———anceſtors more madly fought.

Line 43.———gilds old *Andrea's* ſpires,—dele *old*.

Line 55.———old *Amphion's* ſong,—dele *old*.

                                       Line

Line 62.—Which brave *Matthias* :—Mr Matthew Dunning precentor and seffion-clerk of St Cuthbert's, and brother to Mr Alexander Dunning mentioned above.

Line 72.———its *rapid* courfe,

———its *fteady* courfe.

C A N T O   III.

Line 12.—*Vernon :* Admiral Vernon ;

Britannia's glory and the fcourge of *Spain.*

Line 17.—The light-foot *Fairies,* &c.

The *nimble Fairies,* &c.

Line 86. 87. 88.—The panting dam, &c.

The panting dam, and gently ftroak'd the wound :

The touch divine foon eas'd the mother's pain ;

The wife immortals never touch in vain.

ADDENDUM.

ADDENDUM.

Nestor, who fourscore winters hath withstood,
Nestor the generous, debonnair, and good,
Here trips along, and plays with youthful ease,
Instructs, decides, yet never fails to please.

Dr JAMES MACKENZIE, physician in Edinburgh, is the author of the above stanza.—By *Nestor* we are to understand Mr FALCONER of Fesdo, a most accomplished gentleman. The first of these lines is not to be taken in a strictly literal sense; the Doctor only means a wish that his friend might arrive at that advanced period of human life in full possession of all his faculties. Mr FALCONER delighted much in the game of Goff; and was such an adept in it, that he could play off from the Tee, at a full stroke, twelve successive balls, and lay every one of them within the space of two or three club-lengths from one another: He had, perhaps, a greater collection of clubs than any person ever possessed; they amounted to several hundreds.

FINIS.